The Weight Of Emotions

For The Emotional Human In You

Apurva Varma

BookLeaf
Publishing

India | USA | UK

Made with ❤ on the BookLeaf Publishing Platform
www.bookleafpub.in
www.bookleafpub.com

Dedication

I dedicate this book with all my love to my mom, who is and will be always my *first love* forever. My husband, who is always my *consistent support system.* My beautiful and naughty daughter, who brought *more joy* to our lives. My brother whom I call my *right hand* . And my kind hearted and very emotional father, who is the *backbone* of our family.

Preface

Emotions are heavy. They settle in our hearts, linger in our minds, and shape the way we love, lose, and long for connection. '*The Weight of Emotions*' is a collection of poems that explores the depths of relationships- the tenderness of love, the ache of distance, the storm of heartbreak, and the quiet resilience that follows.

Each poem in this book is a reflection of the struggle we face in love: the unspoken words, the lingering memories, the battles fought in silence. Some pieces may resonate with your own experiences, while others may remind you of emotions you thought you had forgotten. Through love and loss, through hope and despair, these verses hold the weight of feelings we often cannot put into words.

This collection is for those who have loved deeply, lost painfully, and yet, found the strength to carry on. May these poems remind you that every emotion, no matter how heavy, has its own beauty- and that even in struggle, there is poetry.

Apurva Varma

Acknowledgements

This book would not exists if I were not a human with *'a working heart'*. I literally thank every relationships of my life, And I thank my emotional intelligence which always surrounds me with overthinking.

Jokes apart! I really thank the people around me who keep motivating me to think and feel so deeply which brings out a writer or a poetess in me.

To your surprise, let me tell you, I've written these poems when my emotions were on the peak and I was diving in the ocean of it. Instead of going here and there I decided to talk and listen to myself and pen down my thoughts.

Special thanks to my readers, whose love for poetry and being hyper-sensitive towards their loving ones make this journey worthwhile. Your support and appreciation are deeply valued.

A lady with a golden heart, Mum

Mum, I want to ask many things to you,
How can you manage so well, chew and blew?

Why didn't you say, you also love to be loved ?
Why didn't you say, you also wanted to be listened ?
Why didn't you say, you also have your dreams?
Why didn't you say, you also wanted to gleam?

Why didn't you say, you also felt tired ?
Why didn't you say, to rest you also desired ?
Why didn't you say, you also wanted to get admired ?
Why didn't you say, you never wanted to get hired ?

Why didn't you say, you had your favorite dish ?
Why didn't you say, you wanted someone to care for
your wish ?
Why didn't you say, you also wanted few leaves ?
Why didn't you say, you also wanted your stress to
relieve ?

Why didn't you say, last night you had fever ?
Why didn't you say, the works were very heavier?
Why didn't you say, the rude words hurt ?
Why you always keep inside your heart ?

Why didn't you say, the world is not full of love ?
Why didn't you say, there are people who love to bluff ?
Why didn't you say, we have to grow ?
Why didn't you say, we have to face adverse although?

Mum, I'm your grown-up child, but I don't posses your skills.
I'm afraid of thrills.
I want to learn the way how you swallow the pain,
I want to learn the way how you never complain.

Please! Teach me the true ways to face this unpredictable world
Teach me through your experiences whatever you observed.
Teach me the techniques to make other choices yours
Teach me the same, the way everything you adore.

Mum, it'll be awful to call you just 'mother'
God has created you to make this world better.
You're godfather, godmother and all the other altogether

There is no relation greater or better than your mother.

I'm sure, in my last birth I've pleased the god a lot
Therefore, he blessed me you as my mum.

And, there are many things which I want to ask to you,
How can you manage so well, chew and blew...?

I wish to be..

Yesterday God came to me
He asked me for a wish.

Carrying tons of emotions,
Filling my heart with joy,
Delivering a big smile on my face,
I said;
I wish to be my father's manifestant
I wish to be my mother's assistant
I wish to be my sister's subsistent
I wish to be in my brother's enlistment.

The almighty said; Oh I see! You wish to be a girl.
Think twice before playing the dice.

Oh please, I don't need your advice
I don't see the dreams of avarice
It's totally my choice
Can't you fulfill this dark bice?

The divine approved my wish, now as a girl I persist.

Congratulations! It's a girl.
Nurse kept me in my mother's lap with these words.
Thunder of emotions came out from my mother's eyes
My father almost jumped with brise.

Days are passing; I am growing
Years and years are passing tip-toeing
And I'm glowing and growing and growing...

Now, I'm a teenager.
My parents never give damn to my gender
Then, all of a sudden someone called 'society' render
I'm pressurized to keep my dreams in a blender
And yes, this time I surrender.

I'm getting device and advice and being told in concise
Not to make my life a dream paradise
And yes, here I'm broken in pieces and slice.

Now, I crossed my teenage and become a lady
My dreams are now hazy
I spent my days like crazy
I can now think for your happiness, as now it's my
ability.

But, wait. Oh my god! My wish has become a tragedy
Why I chose to be a lady
I'm murdered by someone called society
Nobody has shown their humanity
They have proven their mentality
And grasped me as their opportunity.

It's okay. I can't let myself go down.
I'm a girl, nobody can be my clown.
I never wished to be somebody's crown
I just wanted acceptance of my existence as their own
Eventually, someday someone will come and become my
known
He will definitely help me to become renown.

I heard a story in my childhood; a princess had her
prince
Who used to fulfill her dreams even with hints
Is this reality or still a dream
Do I also get the same, who gives wings to my dream ?

Finally, I got my man for the life
I'll show all my nonsense and childishness and let him
recognize
He'll cuddle me and mollycoddle
I'll take short and unsteady steps known as toddle.

Sometimes I'll be his friend and sometimes he'll be mine
Sometimes I'll shower the love as a mother, sometimes
he'll protect me as a father
Sometimes I'll fight like his sister and sometimes he'll
care as my brother
We'll live our life without any bother

I forget all my years and started dreaming again
And why not? After all I got my man.

A man who will give wings to my dream
Who will help me to gleam
We'll together prepare a scheme and with full steam we'll
work for 'my dream' as a team.

Oh wait! I guess again I dreamt beyond his thought
How could he support me if he has not been taught
There's a fault in the way he has been brought
But, what now? I can't drop
I must go beyond imaginations and forethought
I can't make his mind to think broad
I'm sorry. But, I must not applaud the way he has been
brought up!

I wish the god come back to me
I wish I can change my wish
I wish I have thought twice before playing the dice.

I wish I may keep my thoughts
They need not to be dropped
I must not fight for my right.

I don't wish to fight or beg as well
I don't wish to live in a cell
I don't wish to be called demonist
Meanwhile, I hate the word feminist.

I'm done now! Please god come back to me
I wish to change my wish.
You were right, I was wrong
A girl cannot live her life lifelong...

Do Remember

Do remember!
*The days, the months and **the years***
*The moments, the time and **the tears***

Do remember!
*The feeling of being **cheated***
*When someone is extremely **needed***

Do remember!
*The pain and that **grief***
*Something which you cannot even **brief***

Do remember!
*The place where you **stand***
*Everyone around you has **misunderstand***

Do remember!
*There's nothing like **priority***
*And if it is; that's just **orally***

Do remember!
Nobody is **yours**
If you believe on God, remember! neither angels come
to **floors**

Do remember!
The returns of your **doings**
You really deserve that or they know you'll neither ask
nor go for **suing?**

Do remember!
The importance of your **presence**
You're not really meant for their **remembrance**

Do remember!
Everyone has different **mindset**
The worst which you're facing, they've not **faced yet**

Do remember!
The world is **self obsessed**
They've trapped themselves and **arrest**

Do remember!
You have to value your **own**
Otherwise, be ready to be **thrown**

Do remember!

You have to know your **worth**
Nobody is your well-wisher on this **earth**

Do remember!
Blood relation also **fail**
Do you want to test? Just ask them to **take you out of the**
hell

Do remember!
Every relation has its **color**
But, slowly & gradually it turns **pale and discolor**

At last, do remember!
Trust yourself, nothing is **permanent**
Play the tournament, work on betterment, only you
yourself can change your **environment...!**

Dear self,

Dear self,

*Why did you worry for **others**?*
*Others, whom you call your own **soul-soothers**.*

*Why did you care **a lot**?*
*Were you there someday, even in their **thought**?*

*What did you **expect**?*
The love, the bond, the place or the emotions; were all
*these ever **constant**?*

*What did you **imagine**?*
Silly you! Don't you know life changes, you should be in
*your **margin**!*

*Now, what are you **waiting for**?*
*Somebody to come and to treat you **as before**?*

*Dear self, don't **hurt** yourself **anymore**.*

*Don't worry, **expect** or overthink **anymore**.*

Whatever is your own, it will be with you at any cost
*till **last***
*Otherwise, world changes! You can't get even by **asked**.*

*Let them **fight**, let them **blame**,*
*Let them **frame** and let them burn in their own **flame**.*

*You no need to **justify** your **name**;*
*Coz, you were never in a damn **war-game**.*

Arguments** have no **justification
***Obligations** never feel **sensation**.*

*People always believe in **self-declaration***
*Now, stop being in **illusion**, nobody is yours either*
*your **blood relation**.*

*God has not sent you to be a **'super-human'***
*Exfoliate yourself, burst out and **shout loud**.*

Shout-out all the things whatever you've felt and gone
*through in the **storm cloud***
And tell everyone, you just whished for that constant
*love which was always present in your **domain**.*

*But, wait! Did you forget, you're already proven **culprit**.*
*They've already **judged** and **flushed it**.*

*What? Are you still there **stuck**?*
*Oh my dear self, then that's your **bad luck**.*

*You're precious to yourself, feel your worth and value **by***
doing
*Don't consume the toxins and stop **destroying**.*

*Dear self, stop **expecting**, **worrying** and **waiting***
*You remained **unchanged**, otherwise everything around*
*is **changing**!*

I Love You The Most

I spent so many years in search of peace, patience, love
& life
I didn't find anyone beside.
I was tired, dull & divide
It feels like, something is cutting with a sharp knife.

I was in search of a reason to live,
I was expecting someone to believe.
Someone, who just come to me and never leave
Someone, who just hold me forever and relieve.

Then one day, you silently entered in my soul.
Don't know when & how you become my whole.
You make me feel like, there's a lot in life to unroll.
And you; yes you become a reason why I decided to set a
goal.

You're the one who kick starts my day,
You're the one who destroys all the grey.
You are my yesterday, tomorrow and today.

Tell me the most expensive thing of the universe through
which I could pay.

You know, you have a magical touch!
Oh that beauty! I have never seen such.
That beautiful eyes and cheeks having a rich blush
Let me confess one secret, I've a silent crush.

I feel your presence & vibe
That vibe, which I couldn't describe.
That warmth holds my attention and mesmerize
In my brain, heart, blood & soul my love, only you
imbibe.

You gave me a life to survive
And you're the reason why I'm alive
I strongly believe whatever the problems may arise,
You're just right there, beside me to decide, advise and to
make me feel alright.

You may have been a goddess to others.
For me, you're my summers, winters and all the colors.
You may have met a lot of lovers
But, have you ever met a person like me who surrounds
you day & night and continuously utters?

Could you please come to me tonight?

Hold my finger & hug me tight.
Take me along with yourself in your world bright
I wish to go with you to live forever, being out of
everyone's sight.

Hey Listen, take this note
That I love you the most.
For you, I'm always ready to devote.

Just one thing, never leave me or make me apart from
you, not even as a joke.
And listen; take this note
It's true that I love you the most.

Self Love

Gift yourself with abundance

Surround yourself with peace

Nurture yourself with love & care
Work for your health

Promote your mental well-being

Please yourself with beautiful appearance

Give yourself challenge everyday to be happy in
whatever circumstances

Live your life at the fullest, as today is the last day

Embrace yourself, hug yourself, adore yourself

Ask yourself for the gift it wants from you

Invest your time in your healing

Make an agreement with yourself to keep yourself happy in every state

Promise your mind to never give up

Go on date night with yourself

Feed your stomach with the most tempting dish it wants to have

Analyze your mind and work on your heart

And manifest for your over-all wellness

Give yourself abundance and love which you deserve.

I will meet you!

I'll meet you somewhere someday

May be here or there or somewhere else
I've heard of multiverse
Do you believe in the process of universe?

I'll come with all my perfections and imperfections
You ignore all, and just love me without any rejections.

This time when I'll come
I wouldn't carry any caste, creed or religion
We will make our tiny world out of the people's vision.

I'll come with my list of wishes and choices
Will you quit on me, or resolve the issues with your
kisses?

Take you time to think on the speeches
Don't do quick promises, and create stresses.

I strongly believe in affirmation
But, you must take charge of our foundation.
Because once I come, there will be no probation.

I will enter in your life and take the in-charge-ship of
your sentiments
Trust me! I'll never ask for amendments.
You can't resist to hold yourself from my attachments
Are you ready for all those commitments?

Because,
I will meet you somewhere, someday
May be here or there or somewhere else..

Roller Coaster

Whenever I am unable to gather myself,

Then once, hiding from everyone,

I cry bitterly.

Neither do I scream nor make noise,

I just let the pain of my heart flow in tears.

Some pains cannot be told,

Some pains are only yours,

Only for you to bear,

Even by telling it to someone else,
Your mind doesn't become peaceful.

The mind needs solitude,

A peaceful place to empty itself,

Whenever it becomes very heavy.

Staying on the surface of a false smile,

It becomes like a dust which is eager to come out,

And by flowering in tears,

It becomes absolutely peaceful.

As if someone has cleared a place full of thrones,

And made an empty field,

As if after the upheaval of a storm,

The seas become absolutely peaceful,

As if after a light rain,

The earth becomes satisfied.

Just in the same way,
The heaviness of the mind is emptied.

I am getting comfortable again in my daily routine..
Anyway....

I Love You

The **first sight** *was not so intense,*
Don't know how and when it becomes so much dense.
My mind and heart went through a fence,
Which **takes away** *all my sense.*

This was something new which never happened to me before.
Wait wait! Give me sometime, atleast to explore and restore.
Oh! Why are you looking at me, **standing at the seashore***?*

And what if, I generate my expectations,
Which leads me towards the frustrations
No, I don't want to die in **obligation** *of any relation.*

Okay! I do believe you are different and distinctive
I am falling for you everyday and getting addictive
Now between us, **just love** *is the only objective.*

Now, I have many reasons to love you the way I love
I have my feelings & emotions, which are enough to
make me blush
I have thunder inside me which dive in a rush.

Ah! Never ask me for your flaws,
You've never given me the cause
I can just look at you and applause.

*Your sweet gestures are enough to **turn me on***
No, I wouldn't miss a moment even to breathe, blink or
yawn,
*And if by chance, I fail to receive, I fight the **universe** and*
have withdrawn.

I have heard people saying, love has no boundaries
*Every love story is a **masterpiece to cherish.***
Every journey has breeze and memories,
***Love is the only reason** to love and live for centuries.*

Human Instead of Woman

Don't take yourself as woman
Because, first of all, you are a **human**.

Don't wait for someone to come,
And make you feel like home.

Don't expect from anyone to treat you as queen,
My darling, the whole world is very mean.

Don't fall for dreamy promises,
They're just fictionally glorious.

Don't allow someone else to love you,
Sweetheart, you yourself is a virtue!

Don't let your dreams die,
It's always a high time to fly.

Don't kill your aspiration and ambition.
Keep note, You're also on a mission!

Don't allow your soul to live in inconvenience,
It has also feelings, let it face the world and experience.

Don't live in suffocation,
You have already faced the bifurcation.

Don't permit people to be judgemental,
In the process of proving, you would be left behind being
mental.

Don't wait for anyone to help you in your dream,
It's totally yours, get up beam & gleam!

Don't treat yourself as whole & sole,
People have options, you're just under their control.

Don't make yourself over-burdened,
You're already crushed and worsened.

So, my lovelies!
Live your loved season
Don't let go your dreams frozen
Don't lock up soul in prison
Don't take the authority of being superwoman
Because **Remember, first of all you are a human !**

Too Much

Don't take too much of love,
Be prepared to see the world above

Don't take too much of bond,
Respond your feelings beyond

Don't take too much of emotions,
It makes your life troublesome

Don't take too much of sentiments,
It breaks you in pieces and asks for betterment

Don't take too much of morals,
It later realizes you to live among immorals

Don't take too much of ethics,
People will force you more to doubt on your abilities

Don't take too much of guilt,
World wants you to break and never rebuilt

Don't take too much of awareness,
Tell me about a place where you see fairness

Don't take too much of relationship,
You would be alone in the entire battleship

Don't take too much of stress,
Your near & dear ones would wish for more, and bless

Don't take too much of happiness,
Your life has always a void and there will be emptiness

Don't take too much of care,
Everyone carries multiple faces, beware!

Don't take too much of negligence,
You will start lacking your excellence

Don't take too much of freedom,
You may destroy your wisdom

Don't take too much of boundaries,
People will put you down on knees, and squeeze with ease

Don't take too much of dreams,

Only dreaming will never open your streams

Don't take too much of ambition,
It is simply of no use, without planning for a strong
mission

Don't take too much of laziness,
Obviously you are strengthening your weakness.

Just don't take too much !

I would die...

"I would die for my family"

Okay, but...

Would you exercise for them ?

Would you prioritize your mental health for them?

Would you fix your sleep habits for them?

Would you chase your dreams for them?

Would you quit your bad habits for them?

Would you eat healthy for them?

Would you pick spirituality for them?

Would you pick yourself a right partner for them?

Would you learn to stand after falling for them?

Would you stop materializing your life for them?

Would you be expressive for them?

Would you be expressive & out spoken for them?

*Instead of dying, would you **Live** for them?*

Silent Crying

Have you heard of silent crying?

It's bit uncommon

Crying is usually very loud & audible
But, this is something quiet & inaudible.

You cannot hear it loud,
Only you can feel it's impact.

It comes only when you're unheard, misunderstood and
ill-treated.

When your emotions have been crushed since a long
time,
When all your efforts come to and end

When you become spellbound to narrate something to
someone

When you die everyday while living.

It takes away your mental health first and then ruin you physically

It becomes acute, then cronic, and turns into severe pain

The pain which only can be felt by you

You feel suffocated, breathlessness and numbness in body

Have you faced all these and still surviving and living?

Won't you gave up your life?

Have you tried to live and live more everyday instead of planning to die?

Then you're very brave to lead this life.

You need to stop harming yourself more due to others

Start healing and leaving.

Leaving people, place even memories

Memories which are affecting you every now and then

Get up and keep yourself away from these evil spirits

Get up and gather all your broken pieces

And reform & rebuild yourself

You deserve to be happy
You deserve to live happily!

Emotionally Unavailable

Don't call him emotionally unavailable,
He always supports you being invisible,
He does everything to make you stable,
He's self-sufficient and capable,
But, priorities you and opt to be unexplainable

Yes, he forgets very occasional,
Cannot express being conversational,
Prefers to go sometimes unobtainable,
Sometimes chooses to be non-traceable,
But, he's always available for being transformational.

It's okay, if sometimes he's unavailable,
His qualities are yet not scalable,
His unnoticed efforts are debatable,
He's always gentle towards you and tolerable,
He never treats you as replaceable.

He believes his bond is unbreakable,
He streched himself upto extent to keep you unshakable,

His decisions for you are always infallible,
He bleed to work to make you live comfortable,
Do you still prefer to call him emotionally unavailable?

He & She

He is body, She is soul
He is strength, She is power
He is mind, She is heart

He builds a house
She makes it home

He works to earn money
She works to bring livelihood

He eats to fuel his body
She cooks to feed his body

He has the strength of his mind
She has the strength of her heart

He rules with his thoughts
She overpowers with her emotions

He handles her sentiments

She handles his strains

He supports to let her live her dreams
She encourages to let him dream

They are interdependent !
They are one !
He is she, She is he !

Purpose of life

Hide yourself from the world,
But, always take a tour to your inner world.

Stand in front of the mirror,
Dare to watch yourself clearer.

Bombard yourself with questions,
Prepare yourself beforehand for the digestion.

Reflect on your soul,
It will never make you fool.

When you clearly get the answers,
Start working just like the freelancers.

Don't think too quick about the end,
Attend sincerely and first try to amend.

You don't need any supervisor,
You are more wiser and always your best advisor.

Once you've treated yourself successfully and healed,
Create a better world for others as you dreamed.

Believe your life's journey is successful,
Only when you provide bountiful and will be grateful !

A love letter to myself !

Dear me, I see you.

I see the strength in your heart,
Kindness in your soul.
I see the wat you love others,
The way you give so freely,
Even when you don't always receive in return.

I see you as the sweetest while giving,
And the rudest while dealing to yourself.

I see you going to the end of the world if you care for
them,
Without thinking or caring of your extent.

I want you to know that this kindness is a reflection of
your inner self.
You too deserve the same love, that same care, every
single day, without a second thought or even a doubt.

*You are your first love, safest place and source of your
light.*

*Put yourself first, take gentle care of your heart
Give yourself abundance, don't treat your life as burden*

*For everytime you feel
You're not enough or as if you don't deserve
You should know that
You're far from either of those things & to be loved by
you is not something everyone deserves.*

Remember when ?

*I love the question that begins with **'remember when'**.*
Remember when we sat in the library holding our hands
together while learning?
Remember the warmth when we sat closer to each other
for the very first time?
Remember when I used to wrap my hands around your
arms while watching movies?
Remember when we walk on the streets for hours and
hours without any work?
Remember when we used to skip from everyone's eyes
just to spend few hours together?
Remember when we cried bitterly on our very first fight?
Remember when I cried on your shoulders while
thinking about my mom?
Remember when I was standing there to cherish your
success on the biggest day of your life?
Remember when we struggled together to live together?
Remember when my parents trusted you and said to take
care of me during my newly established life?

Remember when we last sat together to cherish the memories together?

Remember when ?

Desires

There is always a dying patient who wants to live his life

There is always an orphan who wants to have parents

There is always a failure who wants to taste success

There is always an unemployed who wants at least a job for his survival

There is always a mother who wants her children to be immortal

There is always a father who wants his children to be on the top by whatever means

There is always a soldier's wife who waits for a love letter from her husband who died

There is always a lover who wants to be loved the way he deserves

There is always a list of wanting things we cannot get

There is always a god listening and refusing our prayers.

Hey Boy!

Hey boy you deserve

Deserve a gentle care

Fingers on your hair

A deep conversation

A soft kiss on cheeks

A warm hug while leaving

A lap to rest your head

A bowl of meal to taste

A hand to wipe your tears

A strong shoulder to rest your stress

A voice which assures you everything will be alright

A handwritten love note

A red rose

A surprise birthday celebration

A non-judgmental secret keeper

An always available kind of person to call during depression

An unexpected cold email

An unexpected cup of coffee while working

An intense look which says I'll be with you always

Boy like you deserve all the Sun shines,

Don't settle for less,

Hey boy you deserve all !

Blooming

And then one day, I decided to blossom

Leaving all the guilts behind
I choose to live my life

Slowly & gradually releasing the emotions
Which made me over-burdened

I started accepting the truths
Instead of modifying it

I started working on myself
Rather than correcting others

I started omitting the toxicity
And being selective about the things to imbibe

I got convinced nothing lasts forever
So accepted this happily, and moved forward

I took my time as much as I wanted
Because the comeback must not carry the setback

I recollected my pieces myself
And rebuilt a refined version of me

I agreed to the fact of life
Everything is pre-planned and destined

I hugged the flaws of the world
I am part of it, nothing could be perfect

And then one day, I decided to be a flower
Choose to blossom and spread my fragrance